FINER NOBLE GASES

Adam Rapp

BROADWAY PLAY PUBLISHING INC
New York
www.broadwayplaypublishing.com
info@broadwayplaypublishing.com

FINER NOBLE GASES
© Copyright 2005 by Adam Rapp

All rights reserved. This work is fully protected under the copyright laws of the United States of America. No part of this publication may be photocopied, reproduced, stored in a retrieval system, or transmitted, in any form or by any means, electronic, mechanical, recording, or otherwise, without the prior permission of the publisher. Additional copies of this play are available from the publisher.

Written permission is required for live performance of any sort. This includes readings, cuttings, scenes, and excerpts. For amateur and stock performances, please contact Broadway Play Publishing Inc. For all other rights contact the author c/o B P P I.

1st printing: October 2005
I S B N: 978-0-88145-266-2

Book design: Marie Donovan
Word processing: Microsoft Word
Typographic controls: Xerox Ventura Publisher 2.0 P E
Typeface: Palatino
Printed and bound in the U S A

An earlier version of FINER NOBLE GASES premiered in the 2002 Humana Festival of New American Plays at the Actors Theater of Louisville.

This version of FINER NOBLE GASES opened on 20 September 2004, produced by Rattlestick Theater (David Van Asselt, Artistic Director; Sandra Coudert, Managing Director). The cast and creative contributors were:

GRAY .... Connor Barrett
STAPLES .... Robert Beitzel
LYNCH .... Michael Chernus
SPEED .... Ray Rizzo
CHASE .... Paul Sparks

Director .... Michael John Garcés
Scenic design .... Van Santvoord
Costume design .... Elizabeth Hope Clancy
Sound design .... Eric Shim
Production stage manager .... Doug Shearer
Assistant stage manager .... Amber Womack
Assistant director .... Hayley Finn
Assistant costume designer .... Miro D Bullo

CHARACTERS

GRAY
STAPLES
LYNCH
SPEED
CHASE
PETE

(*A filthy East Village apartment near Tomkins Square Park. A typical pre-war Skinner box. A naked window leading to a fire escape. A neon beer sign, turned off. A half-collapsed, stained and bucket-seated sofa, duct tape over the cushions. A coffee table with three glass bowls of pills: a bowl of blue pills; a bowl of pink pills; a bowl of yellow pills. The bowls are neatly arranged. A T V on the floor. A random, street-plucked chair. An equally random ottoman. A full drum set on a homemade, one-foot platform, a microphone stand and mic next to the drum set. An electric and a bass guitar propped on guitar stands. A bass amp. A few guitar amps. Two or three microphone stands set up with mics. Some random cords and wires snaking indecipherably. Sweat socks, junk mail, crumpled beer cans, old set lists, pizza boxes, pools of things here and there. Drifts of debris. A virus of MacDonald's Happy Meal boxes stapled to the wall. A hallway leading to unseen bedrooms. A front door. A small T V surveillance monitor housed in the wall next to the door. Over the monitor, someone has scrawled "MIKE" in black indelible ink.*)

(CHASE *and* STAPLES, *thirtyish, are sitting on the sofa, watching T V. They wear wrinkled thrift-store clothes. They are fully bearded and they smell. There is the feeling that the two of them have been living on the sofa since the previous spring.* STAPLES *sits very still.* CHASE *fidgets a bit, his feet never touching the floor.*)

(*Next to the chair, is* MAN ON THE FLOOR. *He is neither sleeping nor thinking. He is thirtyish, bearded, and lives in his underwear. Someone has written all over him with a black marker.*)

(The only source of light is the blue throb of the TV and a yellowish glow from the back of the apartment where lights have been left on. The noise of the TV should play throughout, but barely audible; an animal being tortured.)

STAPLES: I had this dream last night that I was a robot. Big metal robot. I was crying but nothing was coming out. I could feel the crying. In my throat. But no tears. And I didn't have any balls. Instead I had a light switch. I kept trying to turn it on but all it did was make this buzzing noise.

(CHASE puts his hand down his pants.)

CHASE: Wow.

STAPLES: I know, right?

(They watch.)

CHASE: You do the blues or the pinks?

STAPLES: The blues.

CHASE: The pinks are good. You shouldn't do more than two. Never do more than two. I think some guy did four once.

STAPLES: Whoa.

CHASE: *(Removing his hand)* I know, right?

STAPLES: Halfs or fulls?

CHASE: Fulls.

STAPLES: What happened to him?

CHASE: He got on a bus. The M-15, I think. Tied the driver to a pole and drove through yellow lights all the way to the Upper East Side, got out, ran to the Ninety-Second Street Y, ripped off all his clothes, jumped in the pool.

STAPLES: He did four?

CHASE: Four pinks, yep.

STAPLES: ...Did he have a gun or something?

CHASE: Gunless.

STAPLES: Wow.

CHASE: I know, right?

STAPLES: Could he like swim?

CHASE: Good question.

(They watch.)

STAPLES: I took two once.

CHASE: Pinks?

STAPLES: Uh-huh.

CHASE: Halfs or fulls?

STAPLES: Fulls.

CHASE: Two full pinks?

STAPLES: One right after the other.

CHASE: When?

STAPLES: Coupla days ago.

CHASE: Was I around?

STAPLES: Yeah, you were around.

CHASE: Do you remember where?

STAPLES: You were in your room with that plastic thing.

CHASE: Oh. Right on.

(They watch.)

CHASE: Anything weird happen?

STAPLES: Tried to steal a Christmas tree.

CHASE: Whoa.

STAPLES: I know, right?

CHASE: Like *steal* steal?

STAPLES: Like theft, dude.

CHASE: Where?

STAPLES: New K-Mart by the Six Train.

CHASE: They serve breakfast there. Eggs and stuff.

(They watch.)

CHASE: You get caught?

STAPLES: Yeah. Two undercover security guards. They were cool.

(They watch.)

CHASE: What kinda tree was it?

STAPLES: It was a blue tree, Chase. Smelled like chewing gum.

(They watch.)

CHASE: Blue like what kinda blue?

STAPLES: Blue like when the tape pops out of the V C R blue. Kinda violety.

CHASE: Nice imagery, Staples.

STAPLES: Thanks, Chase.

(They watch.)

STAPLES: I thought it would look good next to the percussion unit. Some lights. A wreath maybe.

CHASE: They got wreaths over at the hardware store on Seventh.

STAPLES: The one with all the paint.

CHASE: Little Green wreaths.

STAPLES: We coulda got one and painted it blue.

CHASE: To match the tree.

STAPLES: And the pills.

(They watch.)

CHASE: It's cool that it was scented.

STAPLES: I know, right?

(They watch.)

STAPLES: Sometimes you look at something. You weigh it in your mind. Like a rock. Or a gallon of paint. French coins are like that.

CHASE: Francs.

STAPLES: Yeah, stuff in your pocket feels better when it's heavy... But the really weird thing...

CHASE: Yeah?

STAPLES: The really weird thing is that I like wanted to get caught.

CHASE: You wanted it.

STAPLES: I did, Chase, I did. I thought maybe they'd yell at me. Stuff like *(As if invaded) Stand up Straight!* Or *Look at me when I'm talking to you!*

CHASE: Did they?

STAPLES: Nu-uh.

CHASE: What'd they do?

STAPLES: They put me in a room. There was this big mirror. A few metal chairs. This woman came in and gave me a glass of water. Then she put the tree up and left me alone with it. I think they were studying me on the other side of the mirror.

CHASE: Like *studying* studying?

STAPLES: Uh-huh.

CHASE: What do you think they were studying?

STAPLES: Probably my mind. The like waves and stuff.

CHASE: Huh.

(They watch.)

CHASE: Did the woman like do anything to the tree after she put it up?

(STAPLES thinks.)

STAPLES: Um. I don't think I understand your question, dude.

CHASE: I don't know. I guess I'm asking about ornaments and stuff. Popcorn. Like did she *decorate* it.

STAPLES: Nu-uh.

CHASE: Huh. *(They watch.)*

STAPLES: It was pretty weird. Lonely.

CHASE: Did like *you* do anything?

STAPLES: Um. Uh-uh. I *felt* like doing something, though. Like getting up and whirling my arms. Or just jumping up and down a few times.

CHASE: Did you get busted?

STAPLES: Busted and disgusted. I called Frank the Father. He called his lawyers. They took care of it.

CHASE: Frank the Father's a lawyer, too, isn't he?

STAPLES: Lawyer. Banker. C F O. U F O.

CHASE: Unidentified Flying... Financial Officer.

(STAPLES imitates a U F O flying through the air CHASE follows it with an invisible ray gun, shoots it. They both follow its decent to the earth and watch it crash, laugh sadly.)

(One of them farts like a French horn.)

CHASE: Was that you or me?

STAPLES: I think it was you.

CHASE: Oh.

(They watch.)

STAPLES: I think about doing stuff but I get tired. Like more stealing. Canned fish. Little plastic things. Gum.
  Or breaking a window with my *fist*! Wrapping it with the newspaper first and then *punching!* Or kicking a garbage can!

(CHASE starts to twitch uncontrollably.)

STAPLES*(Calm now)* Dude, you're like twitching all over the place.

(CHASE twitches.)

STAPLES: That's so cool. I wish I could twitch...
  Sometimes I'll look at my hand. Like at a finger. And I'll say to it, I'll say *Move*. And it will.

CHASE: Motor skills.

STAPLES: That's how aliens must do stuff. I mean if they're in a human body. Cause they don't have the muscle memories. So they have to tell themselves what to do. Hands and feet. Arms. They'll say *Walk legs*. Like in their language. They'll command themselves to do it. And they'll just start walking places. So there's more lag time with aliens. Cause they don't have the memories.

(CHASE's twitching punctuates into an explosive bicep muscle.)

CHASE: Feel my muscle.

STAPLES: Feel your muscle?

CHASE: Yeah.

STAPLES: Like *feel* feel it?

CHASE: Sure.

STAPLES: No way, dude.

CHASE: Come on, Staples, covet my power source! Feel the way my calories burn with whitehot fire!

STAPLES: That's way too close, Chase!

CHASE: Whitehot, blistering foxfire!!!

STAPLES: All I ask for is two feet!

CHASE: The truth of my muscle would crush thee!!! *(He releases his muscle. Catching his breath)* You feel so much on the pinks. So much feeling.

STAPLES: The blues are cool, too.

CHASE: The blues give you the blues. Like someone's inside you playing a harmonica.

STAPLES: Someone really really small.

(They watch.)

CHASE: Yeah. And then there's the pissers.

STAPLES: The pissers give you the runs.

CHASE: But they make you feel stuff.

STAPLES: Oh, they're total feelwhores.

CHASE: Like the pinks but quicker.

STAPLES: A little hotter, too. Like plants.

CHASE: Like plants?

STAPLES: Yeah, plants. Like in a greenhouse. How they do that thing to the Sun. Trap it or something.

CHASE: ...Photosynthesis.

(The front door opens. LYNCH enters, closes the door. He is thirty, big, heavily bearded. He wears layers and layers of old sweats, batting gloves, a scarf, a dockworker's skullcap, construction boots, a weight belt, a small white mask over his nose and mouth. He is exhausted, hunched, slow moving. He

*carries a cheap metal space heater, drops it on the floor.
There is the sense that he has to search for every step.
While crossing he stops behind the sofa and is lured by
the TV. He watches. Only the sound of the shrieking animal.)*

*(After a moment, LYNCH takes a few long strides toward the
TV and then kicks it in.)*

*(The MAN ON THE FLOOR rises and crosses upstage.
He takes his underwear down and begins urinating
thoroughly into a broken tom-tom drum.)*

*(LYNCH turns, stares at CHASE and STAPLES for a moment
and exits to the back of the apartment, closes a door.)*

*(CHASE and STAPLES stare at the kicked in TV, while the
MAN ON THE FLOOR continues to urinate.)*

STAPLES: Chase?

CHASE: Yeah, Staples?

STAPLES: I don't know what to like um *do*. ...I'm getting up!

CHASE: Yeah?

STAPLES: Yeah, I'm getting up! *(He doesn't move.)*

CHASE: Maybe count to three or something.

STAPLES: Good idea.

CHASE: I'll count for you.

STAPLES: Okay.

CHASE: Ready?

STAPLES: Yeah, I'm ready. Go head.

CHASE: One. Two. Three.

*(STAPLES rocks himself forward and off the sofa. He lurches
slightly, rights himself.)*

*(The MAN ON THE FLOOR finishes urinating, pulls his
underwear up, crosses to a spot near the chair, lies down.)*

CHASE: You okay?

STAPLES: Yeah, yeah, I'm good.

(STAPLES *turns and crosses to the front door like some kind of lost and forlorn spaceman. He stares at the surveillance monitor and then lifts his arm and turns it on. It issues a vague, bluish-white screen, a few obscure lines.* STAPLES *attempts to wave the light from the monitor toward the T V, as if it will somehow cause it to work again.* CHASE *joins him and they wave with great fervor. They stop and watch the T V for a moment.*)

CHASE: It's not working.

STAPLES: Not really, right?

CHASE: Nu-uh.

(STAPLES *crosses back to the sofa, sits.*)

STAPLES: We could like watch Mike the Monitor.

CHASE: We could.

STAPLES: Maybe we should move the davenport. Make it easier to see.

CHASE: Good idea.

(*They stare at each other a moment.*)

STAPLES: One. Two. Three.

(STAPLES *rolls over his arm of the sofa and begins budging it toward the monitor.* CHASE *never actually gets off the sofa and attempts to move it by using whatever force he can generate by charging and ramming into one of its arms. They surf-scoot-pivot the sofa so that it faces the surveillance monitor.* STAPLES *sits back down, exhausted. They watch the monitor.*)

CHASE: It's not bad.

STAPLES: Not too bad.

CHASE: I like how it's kinda blank.

STAPLES: Yeah. The blankness.

CHASE: It's like snow.

STAPLES: It is kinda.

CHASE: Like a little box of snow.

STAPLES: A little box fulla snowballs.

(They watch.)

CHASE: But it's not the same!

STAPLES: I know, right?!

CHASE: I keep expecting things!

STAPLES: Yeah, Chase, me too!

CHASE: Like a little caribou to appear!

STAPLES: I know, I know!

CHASE: And the rhino!!

STAPLES: How those birds were just sitting on his back like someone put em there!!

(They stare at each other.)

CHASE: One. Two. Three.

(STAPLES *rises off the sofa, and return it to its original position. Again,* CHASE *never actually touches the floor and uses the same charging-ramming method. After the sofa is re-positioned, they sit, exhausted.)*

(CHASE *suddenly charges to* STAPLES' *end of the sofa, violently pukes over the side, smothering* STAPLES *with his body. After a moment, he thaws from the hurling, wipes his mouth, returns to his side.)*

CHASE: Should I call Doug the Dad?

STAPLES: Call Doug the Dad. If it doesn't work I'll call Frank the Father.

(CHASE *starts to burrow in the cracks of the sofa, searching for his cell phone. After a moment, he realizes that it is on the chair.* STAPLES *reaches into his pocket, lends him his cell phone.* CHASE *attempts to dial the number, but can't remember it. He hands the cell phone back to* STAPLES *and then lunges for the coffee table rather Olympically, and then, without ever touching the ground, manages to traverse the space between the sofa and the chair, using whatever means necessary: the coffee table, the ottoman, etc. It should be an enormous feat. He winds up securing his cell phone semi-miraculously, sits on the ottoman, speed dials, waits.)*

CHASE: Hey, Daddy? It's Chase... Hey Daddy. How's it going? How's business?... Good, good...

What do I want? Well, nothing, Daddy. Just calling to say Hey. Hey and how's it going and how's Mary the Mom and all that...

Oh, things are great. Really great.

Yeah, it's getting cold out, I think. Pretty cold. Scarves and mittens, you know?...

Oh the band is so good. It's been a real productive period. We're writing songs like crazy... Oh, everything. Vocals. Rhythm guitar. Some very clever leads now and then. Keyboards. A little drums here and there, rat-a-tat-tat, percussion, you know? I'll send you a tape... Sure, sure... Yeah, I got the check. I totally got it. Yeah, thanks, Daddy...

Well, there was one thing, Daddy. One small thing... Yeah... Yeah, I know... Well, it's pretty small, small as a kittycat, but it's important. Really really kinda huge and important... Well, our T V got messed up somehow... Yeah, the old Trinitron... Well, I don't know. It's like there's a big hole in it... In the screen... Well not a *hole* hole, more like a black um *void*. Yeah, a black void in the middle...

Could I maybe like use the credit card?... I know, I know... Well, we do need it, Daddy. Cause we're thinking about shooting a video... Yeah... And we need

something to watch it on. I could just buzz over to the Wiz, you know? They got great deals over there. They might even deliver.
(*He nods to* STAPLES, *smiles*).
  No?... Oh... You sure, dude? Okay. Okay, Daddy... Yeah, I'm working. Working on the music, you know? Art's a full-time job. No compensation yet, but there will be. Big things ahead. Nothing but the sky...
  Yeah, sure I'll come home for a few days... Maybe next month... I'll just jump on the Metro North. A little Northbound train action.
  Okay, Daddy... Me, too... Tell Mom I say Hey... I know, I know... Sure...I'll send that tape off.
(*He turns the phone off, slips it back into his pocket.*)
  Your turn, dude. Frank the Father.

(STAPLES *dials his cell phone, waits. After a moment he starts to make pig sounds into the phone. Pigs, monkeys, and sheep. He stops, turns the phone off, puts it back in his pocket, looks at* CHASE.)

CHASE: Voicemail?

(STAPLES *nods.*)

(*The sound of a door closing. Moments later,* LYNCH *appears from the back of the apartment. He is dressed in camouflage winter hunting wear. He steps slowly into the room as though he isn't sure where he is heading, stands very still.*)

CHASE: Alaska man.

STAPLES: Man Alaska.

CHASE: What's with the outerwear?

LYNCH: It's gettin cold.

CHASE: Yeah?

LYNCH: Sposed to get in the teens tonight.

STAPLES: Whoa.

CHASE: Better turn the heat up.

LYNCH: Things aren't workin out so well. It's better if there's snow when that happens.

(CHASE *and* LYNCH *stare at each other.*)

CHASE: Where you goin, dude?

LYNCH: Get somethin for my toe.

CHASE: What's wrong with your toe?

LYNCH: It's numb.

CHASE: Like *numb* numb?

LYNCH: Uh-huh.

STAPLES: It's prolly from the T V.

LYNCH: Meaning?

STAPLES: Oh, nothing. It's just that you like totally kicked it in and such.

LYNCH: Felt like the right thing to do. The perfect time, you know? *(As if invaded)* IT'S MONSTER MADNESS AT THE KIEL AUDITORIUM BIG TRUCKS *BIG BIG* TRUCKS TRUCKS SO BIG OTHER TRUCKS CAN RIDE AROUND INSIDE OF THEM!!!

(The explosion sends LYNCH *across the room, somewhere near drum set. He stares at it confused for a second.)*

LYNCH: *(A reaching out)* I feel really far away from things. Like everything's gettin smaller.

(Nobody moves.)

CHASE: Um. How was like work, dude?

LYNCH: Okay.

CHASE: What kinda stuff you move?

LYNCH: Sofas. Bookcases. Beds. Some statues.

CHASE: Like *statue* statues?

LYNCH: Men, Women. Men mostly.

STAPLES: Were they like nude?

LYNCH: Yeah.

STAPLES: Any hot bods?

(LYNCH *reaches into one of his pocket and removes a marble breast.*)

STAPLES: *Dude.*

CHASE: *Dude!* Gettin a little on the side!

(LYNCH *starts to slowly move the breast through the air, almost dancing with it. He hums a melodious tune.* CHASE *and* STAPLES *collaborate a bit.* LYNCH *blows into the breast as if it is a conch shell, making his way toward* CHASE. *He places the breast on* CHASE's *head, his face, his beard. What seems like fun starts to get a little scary as he uses the marble breast to force* CHASE's *head into the cushion of the chair.*)

LYNCH: *(Releasing* CHASE's *head)* Can't have it!

CHASE: Cool.

LYNCH: *(To* STAPLES*)* You either!

STAPLES: Hey, that's totally cool.

(LYNCH *puts the marble breast back in his pocket.*)

LYNCH: I used to know a lot more stuff.*(To* CHASE*)* When we were in school, you know?

CHASE: Sure.

LYNCH: Facts mostly. I was good with facts.

CHASE: Facts are good.

STAPLES: Yeah, dude. Facts are totally good.

LYNCH: I've been keeping a brick in my pocket. Left pocket.

CHASE: A brick and a tit.

LYNCH: Found it in the basement.

CHASE: The basement?

STAPLES: Like the basement basement?

LYNCH: Uh-huh.

CHASE: What were you like doing down in the basement?

LYNCH: Lookin for things. Gettin stuff together.

CHASE: Things?

STAPLES: Stuff?

LYNCH: Things and stuff. Lookin and gettin. Pretty much in that order. *(To* CHASE*)* There's all these robots everywhere.

(STAPLES *tries to make himself invisible.*)

CHASE: Robots?

LYNCH: Uh-huh. Millions of em. A hundred million.

CHASE: Cool.

LYNCH*(To* STAPLES*)* They're just layin there like they're sleepin. A hundred million robots.

(CHASE *and* STAPLES *stare at each other.*)

(LYNCH *turns, crosses to the* MAN ON THE FLOOR. *From his mouth he drops a slow gob of spit on him. The* MAN ON THE FLOOR *doesn't stir.* LYNCH *watches him for a moment and then crosses to the front door. Before he exits, he removes a brick from his left pocket and smashes through the front of the surveillance monitor.*)

LYNCH: *(Another reaching out)* Bye.

CHASE: Bye.

STAPLES: Bye, dude.

LYNCH: Washington was a good president. But Lincoln was better. You can tell cause of the pictures. His beard and stuff.

(LYNCH *exits. His footfalls can be heard descending the stairs.* CHASE *and* STAPLES *sit very still.*)

CHASE: I have an idea.

STAPLES: Yeah?

CHASE: Heldinwell.

STAPLES: *Heldinwell?*

CHASE: The guy who lives downstairs. The weird guy in number three.

STAPLES: What about him?

CHASE: *He's* got a T V.

STAPLES: You're saying?

CHASE: We should totally take it.

STAPLES: Like rob him?

CHASE: Sure. I'll invite him up and while he's under my narrative spell you can use the fire escape and bust into his apartment and snag his T V.

STAPLES: Good idea.

CHASE: I know, right?

STAPLES: Sneaky.

CHASE: It's totally sneaky.

STAPLES: ...So, um, can I like ask a question?

CHASE: Sure.

STAPLES: Why do you get to be the narrative spell guy?

CHASE: Cause, dude, I'm a good conversationalist.

STAPLES: You are?

CHASE: Dude, I'm such a good conversationalist. My words and images. My use of metaphor and freakish nouns.

STAPLES: Are you trying to say that I'm like not good at images and freakish nouns?

CHASE: No.

STAPLES: Cause I can totally paint pictures with words, Chase. You know I'm so good at that.

CHASE: You are, you are.

STAPLES: I'm like a metaphor *fac*tory.

CHASE: *(Secure on the coffee table now)* That's true, Staples. That's totally true. But where you're the factory I'm like the quality control division. I make the metaphor a little more slippery. I add the salt and pepper. The spicy spices. I'm like the quality control *chef* who takes on the metaphor as soon as it comes off the assembly line.

STAPLES: But, dude—

CHASE: Plus, you're on the blues. I'm on the pinks!

STAPLES: I'm such a good conversationalist, Chase. I have a large assortment of words and ideas.

CHASE: Why do you think I like hanging with you so much? Besides, you're the one who's always getting locked out and coming in through the window.

STAPLES: What's that supposed to mean?

CHASE: Nothing. Just that you're more familiar with the ways and means of the fire escape. It's one of the things you're really really good at.

STAPLES: ...Maybe.

CHASE: I'll call him.
(He leaps from the chair lands on his side of the sofa rather

impressively, pulls his cell phone out of his pocket, dials, waits.)

Yes. I'd like the number of a *Heldinwell* on East Tenth Street in Manhattan... Cool.*(He winks at* STAPLES.*)* Hello. Is this Mister Heldinwell?... It is?... Oh, hey. This is Chase. Chase Fitzsimmons, your upstairs neighbor in apartment five...

Hey! How's it going?... Good, good.
Well, anyway, the reason I'm calling is cause I sorta hurt my back real bad today... Yeah, I slipped on the ice and landed on the old sacrosternum... Yeah, slipped and fell like an old person. *Whooop!*... Oh, the sacro*ster*num, that thing under the spinal canal... Yeah, in the lumber division...

Anyway, I'm on these killer pain pills. These big pharmaceutical hockey pucks. And the thing is, I'm feeling a little fuzzed-out and insecure and both my roommates are away for the weekend. You see, I keep thinking someone's behind me. It's pretty bad...

(STAPLES *slowly turns, checks behind the sofa.)*

CHASE: Well, I know it sounds silly, but I was wondering if you wouldn't mind coming upstairs and entertaining me for a while. I keep wanting to turn around real fast but I know I'm not supposed to cause of my discs and stuff. The lumber division of the spinal canal is quite neurologically and anatomically sensitive... You would? Cool, cool. I'd really appreciate that... Yeah, I just thought we could talk for a while. Shoot the breeze, you know? Get to know each other neighbor to neighbor. Upstairs to downstairs. Man to man...

God, I so appreciate that... It's these pills, you know? I think I took too many. I almost broke down and called a film festival—

STAPLES: Dude!

CHASE: I mean *hospital*!... Oh, come up as soon as you can. A S A P. The door's open. Yeah, I keep wanting to turn around. Thanks, guy. I so appreciate it. See you in a few. *(He hangs up.)*

STAPLES: Nice?

CHASE: Oh, totally nice. Kinda shy.

STAPLES: Huh.

(A pause)

CHASE: Um. He's probably like on his way up the stairs right now.

STAPLES: You think it's gonna snow?

CHASE: I don't know, Staples.

STAPLES: I used to make snowmen. Big ones. With hats and stuff. Scarves. I'd sit next to them and we'd memorize baseball cards. Height. Weight. Hometown. We'd do state capitals, too. Albany. Tallahassee. Jefferson City... Do you know the state capital of Illinois?!

CHASE: Sure, Staples.

STAPLES: What is it?!

CHASE: It's Springfield, isn't it?

(STAPLES stares off.)

CHASE: You okay, buddy?

STAPLES: I keep thinking about the caribou. How it reminds me of all this stuff I can't remember. Like being on a school bus. The way the seats smelled. Stuff like that. And Magilla Gorilla!

CHASE: What about him?

STAPLES: I can't remember if he was a walrus or an Alaskan snow pony!!!

CHASE: Um. I think he was a gorilla, Staples.

STAPLES: Yeah?

CHASE: I'm pretty sure about that one.

STAPLES: I was thinking about getting a job today. Doing something with my hands. Catching fish. Making things. Little wooden toys.

CHASE: Toys are cool.

STAPLES: *(A little terrified)* I had this dream last night that I was a robot. Big metal robot—

CHASE: Yeah, you were crying—

STAPLES: I was crying but nothing was coming out. I could feel the crying in my throat but no tears—

CHASE: And you didn't have any balls—

STAPLES: I didn't have any balls. Instead I had a light switch! I kept trying to turn it on—

CHASE: But all it did was make this buzzing noise.

STAPLES: I was going to this graveyard. Where all the other robots were buried. And I found this flower. It was pink. A tulip, I think. I ate it. It made me feel better.

CHASE: Look, if all goes well, I bet we'll get to see what happens to the caribou.

STAPLES: You think so?

CHASE: I *totally* think so.

STAPLES: I'd like that.

CHASE: Me too, Staples. Me too. You want me to count to three?

STAPLES: Would you?

CHASE: Sure, buddy. *(Squaring his body to STAPLES)* One. Two. Three.

(STAPLES *rocks forward and off the sofa, lurches a bit, rights himself, and then stares at the bowls of pills. He goes for a pink.*)

STAPLES: Maybe I should take a pink.

CHASE: I don't know, Staples! Maybe another blue. Keep the colors together.

STAPLES: Right. (*He reaches down, grabs a blue pill, puts it in his mouth, swallows. Then he turns and crosses to the back of the apartment.*)

(CHASE *stretches out on the sofa, his head opposite the front door. He puts a pillow under his knees, affects the posture of a back injury victim. Moments later,* STAPLES *appears wearing a snowmobile suit. He crosses to the stage left window, attempts to lift it. It doesn't budge. He tries again. No luck*)

STAPLES: It's frozen shut.

(*A knock at the door*)

(CHASE *and* STAPLES *stare at each other, stare at the door, back at each other.* STAPLES *tries to lift the window again, screaming now. It still won't budge.* CHASE *shouts at him to hide in the back of the apartment. He uses strange, guttural noises and a kind of primordial gibberish.*)

(STAPLES *moves as quickly as he can down the hall to the back of the apartment, like an astronaut in need of a toilet.*)

(*Another knock*)

CHASE: Come in.

(*The door opens very slowly. A nondescript man enters. He is thirty-ish, clean-shaven. He wears a plain gray suit and a vague tie. He wears, black, thick-rimmed glasses. He carries a half dozen tulips arranged in a glass vase. He leaves the door open. He is painfully shy, but can get into the occasional groove just like anybody else.*

GRAY: Are you Chase?

CHASE: I am. You must be...

GRAY: Um. Gray. Gray Heldinwell. From apartment three.

CHASE: Well, hey there, neighbor.

GRAY: Hey.

CHASE: How's it going?

GRAY: Pretty good.

CHASE: Well, come in, come in.

GRAY: Thanks. *(He closes the door and steps carefully into the room.)*

GRAY: I brought you these.

(He crosses to CHASE, hands him the tulips.)

CHASE: *(Amazed at their vividness)* Flowers!

GRAY: Tulips.

CHASE: Wow. Um. Thanks...*Gray?*

GRAY: Yeah, Gray.

CHASE: ...Hey, Gray!

GRAY: Hey!

(GRAY stands there awkwardly. CHASE stares at the tulips, is strangely transfixed. Perhaps he licks one. GRAY takes them away.)

GRAY: *(Setting them on the T V)* When I was in the hospital Nurse H would always bring me tulips.

CHASE: Nice.

GRAY: Nurse H and I had similar tastes in things. We both like travel literature. And slanted rain. And knives.

CHASE: Knives?

GRAY: Yeah, we both have knife collections.

CHASE: What kinda knives?

GRAY: Nurse H has two dozen Willie Stonetooth Redpoints. I have a set of Captain Diablo Throwing Blades.

CHASE: Wow.

GRAY: You can only get Captain Diablos south of the border. They come in sets of ten. Varying weights and flight speeds.

CHASE: Cool.

(GRAY *continues to stand.*)

CHASE: Be seated earthling.

(GRAY *stares at the empty stage left chair for a moment, then at the* MAN ON THE FLOOR.)

GRAY: I thought you said your roommates were out of town.

CHASE: They are.

GRAY: *(Pointing to the* MAN ON THE FLOOR*)* Who's that?

CHASE: Oh, that's Speed.

GRAY: Speed?

CHASE: Yeah, Speed. He just got here. Surprise visit.

GRAY: Oh. What's he doing?

CHASE: He's just sorta hanging out.

(GRAY *turns toward the door.*)

CHASE: Take a seat!

(GRAY *stops, considers the chair again, sits.*)

GRAY: So how'd you hurt your back?

CHASE: Well, I slipped and... Well, you know... *(A vague gesture)* Whooop!

GRAY: *(Feebly imitating the gesture)* Whooop.

(Pause)

GRAY: That's what I was in the hospital for.

CHASE: What.

GRAY: My back.

CHASE: Really.

GRAY: They almost had to do invasive surgery. Pinched nerve.

CHASE: Ouch.

GRAY: Sciatic node between L-five and S-one. The pain was pretty excruciating. Two days of traction and a few months of physical therapy. I'm okay now.

CHASE: Wow.

GRAY: Yeah, I had to lay on the floor a lot... Did they medicate in triplicate?

CHASE: Um...

GRAY: Anti-inflammatory, muscle relaxer, painkiller?

CHASE: Oh. Well, um, yeah, actually. All of the above.

GRAY: The Carisprodol is pretty good. They give you that?

CHASE: They did. Yes. They *did* give me that.

GRAY: It's great right before bed. Especially coupled with the Hydrocodone. They probably gave you that, too, right?

CHASE: How'd you know?

GRAY: It's good for nerve pain. Hydrocodone's a synthetic narcotic. Generic spin-off of codeine. Well, they say codeine but it's actually closer to morphine.

CHASE: Wow, Gray, you're like pharmacologically blessed.

GRAY: The Naproxin's nothing to write home about, but an anti-inflammatory's an anti-inflammatory. Seen one you've seen them all.

CHASE: You're so right.

GRAY: *(Rising off the crate, crossing toward the sofa)* I still have a pretty good relationship with my orthopedic guy. Doctor P, N Y U Medical Center.

CHASE: Yeah, Doctor P, N Y U Medical. Over there at

GRAY: Thirty-first and First.

CHASE: Thirty-first and first. Right, right.

GRAY: You should be okay in forty-eight to seventy-two hours. As long as it's not a hot disc. You don't have a hot disc do you?

CHASE: Oh, no way. My discs are totally cool and non-hot.

GRAY: Then you're probably in pretty good shape.

CHASE: God I hope so.

(Someone farts like a French horn. Awkward pause)

CHASE: So, how long have you been in the building, Gray?

GRAY: A while. I just signed another lease.

CHASE: You like the neighborhood?

GRAY: Of course.

CHASE: We got the park. The Russian Bath House. That funny hat shop across the street.

GRAY: That hat shop's not funny.

CHASE: Oh. I was just saying—

GRAY: I don't think it's funny at all.

CHASE: Okay.

(Someone farts again.)

CHASE: Was that you or me?

GRAY: I think it was you.

CHASE: Oh.

GRAY: *(Collaboratively)* Maybe it was Speed?

CHASE: Right on.

(They share forced laughter.)

CHASE: Care for a pill? We have blues, pinks, and yellows. We call the yellows pissers.

(GRAY rises, considers the pills for a moment, back away.)

GRAY: No thanks.

(Suddenly, STAPLES appears from the back of the apartment. He is still wearing the snowmobile suit. He is also wearing a hood now and snow goggles. He walks up to the window very quickly, somehow trying to make himself invisible. He tries to lift it again. He is successful this time. He crawls through the window, closes it behind him, and disappears down the fire escape. GRAY is quite startled.)

GRAY: Who was that?

CHASE: Huh?

GRAY: That man.

CHASE: What man?

GRAY: The one in the snowsuit.

CHASE: I didn't see anyone.

GRAY: Oh. Well, a man in a snowsuit just walked through your living room, opened the window and exited down the fire escape.

CHASE: Really?

GRAY: Yeah.

CHASE: Are you sure, dude?

GRAY: Sure I'm sure. *(He rises, crosses toward the window, creeps up on it very slowly, seizes one of the dinette chairs, then looks out quickly. After a moment, he re-sets the chair, crosses to* CHASE.*)* He's not there any more. *(He crosses toward the door.)*

CHASE: Sit, sit, sit!

*(*GRAY *crosses to the living room chair, confused, regards* SPEED *for a moment, sits.* CHASE *shifts to the other side of the sofa. He feigns pain.* GRAY *rises and attempts to help him, awkwardly reaching toward him, but never actually touching him.* CHASE *settles with his head against the stage right side of the sofa, still feigning pain.* GRAY *accidentally falls into* CHASE's *lap face-first.* GRAY *stands very quickly. An awkward moment.* GRAY *attempts to regain his composure, makes his way back to the chair, sits.)*

CHASE: What do you do, Gray?

GRAY: ...Excuse me?

CHASE: What.

GRAY: I'm not gay.

CHASE: Huh?

GRAY: You think I'm gay?

CHASE: Dude, what are you talking ab—

GRAY: *(Standing)* Didn't you just ask me if I was gay?

CHASE: Um, no. I asked you—

GRAY: Are you trying to take advantage of me?!

CHASE: All I said was—

GRAY: CAUSE I WON'T LET THAT HAPPEN! I KNOW KARATE!

CHASE: I *said* WHAT-DO-YOU-DO, GRAY!

GRAY: Oh.

CHASE: WHOA!

GRAY: ...Sorry.

CHASE: NO ONE IS TAKING ADVANTAGE OF ANYONE!

GRAY: Oh...I'm so sorry.

(CHASE *suddenly realizing that he is standing with little effort, begins feigning pain again, crumples down to the sofa.* GRAY *attempts to help him again, but* CHASE *wards him off.*)

(GRAY *turns to the chair, where* SPEED *has managed to drape his arm over the cushion.*)

GRAY: *(Crossing back to the chair)* I work for a prominent financial institution.

CHASE: Like a bank?

GRAY: It's a little more complicated than that.

CHASE: Okay.

GRAY: *(Removing* SPEED's *arm)* I'm involved with the information side of things. Sorting and processing. I deal with data.

CHASE: You crunch numbers.

GRAY: I do. I do crunch numbers. But I do so much more than just crunch them.

CHASE: Like what?

GRAY: Well, I soften them too. I soften *and* crunch. And there's a fair amount of spreading as well.

CHASE: Spreading?

GRAY: Sure.

CHASE: Like spreadsheets?

GRAY: Just spreading.

CHASE: Huh.

(Suddenly, GRAY whirls around in the chair really fast, desperately looks over both shoulders, stops.)

GRAY: You sure you didn't see that guy in the snowsuit?

CHASE: Pretty sure, Gray.

(SPEED suddenly pulls a deflated blowup doll from underneath the cushion of the chair, screams, heads for CHASE, who is already holding a yellow pill.)

CHASE: Yellow, yellow, yellow...yellow.

(SPEED eats the pill out of CHASE's hand, falls back on his ass for a moment, and then climbs to the top of the sofa, screams, and bounds apelike toward the hallway, punches a hole in the Sheetrock.)

SPEED: Magilla Gorilla. *(He crosses to the back of the apartment singing the first few versus of the* Magilla Gorilla *theme song, disappears.)*

(GRAY regains his composure, sets the guitar down, a little invigorated, sits.)

GRAY: *(Referring to SPEED)* You're in a band.

CHASE: I am.

GRAY: I'll bet you didn't think I knew that.

CHASE: Well—

GRAY: When you've lived in the building as long as I have you pick up on certain things. The walls are filled with information, trust me on that one. You just have to know how to listen.

CHASE: Huh.

GRAY: What are you guys called again?

CHASE: Well, we were called Lester's Surprise, but then we changed it to Lester's Sister. And then it was just Lester. I can't remember what we were after that.

GRAY: Less.

CHASE: Excuse me?

GRAY: I think you were called Less after that.

CHASE: Really.

GRAY: Uh-huh.

CHASE: Like less less?

GRAY: L-E-S-S. You guys used to put posters up all over the place. "Less is More."

CHASE: Huh.

GRAY: Yeah, I used to get out some. People to see, places to go, you know?

CHASE: Sure.

GRAY: But not so much lately. Too much to do. Projects. Big plans. Lots of ideas.

CHASE: Huh.

(GRAY *crosses to the tulips.*)

GRAY: I have this lamp. White cut glass. It has a swan's neck. The head is shaped like tulips. Ten of them. A bouquet. Gives a real nice soft glow. An astral glow. I think they put argon gas in the bulbs. At least it says that on the little tag. I found it in that old thrift shop across the street. It hardly cost anything.

CHASE: ...Uh-huh?

GRAY: I'll just stare at it for hours. I'm not sure why. Sometimes I think I'm waiting for it to talk to me. Like the tulips will tell me what to do.

CHASE: Huh.

(Pause)

GRAY: I was approached on the street today.

CHASE: Approached?

GRAY: Yeah, approached. Carefully approached.

CHASE: By who?

GRAY: Two men. Very important men.

CHASE: When you say "approached"—

GRAY: They just emerged. The way birds emerge.

CHASE: Birds.

GRAY: Large, dark birds. You mind if I turn the light off?

CHASE: Not at all.

(GRAY *vigilantly crosses to the neon beer sign, sets a chair to reach it, stands on the chair, turns the sign off.*)

CHASE: So what did these "very important" men *do* after they um "emerged"?

GRAY: *(Still standing on the chair)* Handed me some pamphlets. Took my information.

CHASE: What kinda information?

GRAY: Personal things. Height. Weight. Social Security Number. Stuff like that.

CHASE: Wow.

GRAY: They took a Polaroid, too.

CHASE: Friendly.

GRAY: Yeah, I was wearing my hat.

CHASE: Your hat?

GRAY: From Millie's Millinery.

CHASE: What's that?

GRAY: Um. That hat shop across the street.

CHASE: Right.

GRAY: There's a meeting tomorrow. Big meeting.

CHASE: With those guys who "approached" you.

GRAY: I'm not supposed to talk about it!

CHASE: Okay.

GRAY: They gave me some money.

CHASE: To not talk about it.

GRAY: A lot of money. In a shoebox. It was heavier than if shoes were in it.

CHASE: Cool.

GRAY: I think a certain government official is in danger, let's just say that. And like they said, he deserves to be.

CHASE: Sure.

GRAY: I'm willing to go to certain lengths.

CHASE: Of course.

GRAY: Long Daniel's going to be speaking on Public Access in a few minutes.

CHASE: Who's that?

GRAY: Leader of the movement.

CHASE: One of the "money dudes"?

GRAY: Long Daniel's the visionary. They work for him. He's the guy in all the literature. *(Referring to the T V)* Public Access. Channel Sixteen.

CHASE: I'd turn it on, Gray, but our T V's like totally cashed.

(Suddenly, STAPLES appears in the window with a large T V. CHASE sees him.)

GRAY: Then I'll go get mine.

CHASE: Your T V?

GRAY: Sure.

CHASE: Oh, no, you don't have to do that!

GRAY: But I want to.

CHASE: But it's so inconvenient. And I wouldn't want you to hurt your back agai—

GRAY: You don't like me.

CHASE: Oh, that's so not true!

GRAY: You find me repellent. *(He turns away, hurt.)*

CHASE: Gray. Hey. Hey now. I find you so totally not repellent.

(CHASE *desperately signals to* STAPLES *to take* GRAY's *T V back downstairs.* STAPLES *watches vaguely through the window for a moment, then nods, and disappears.)*

GRAY: *(Rising, regaining his composure)* They don't talk to me at work.

CHASE: They *talk* to you.

GRAY: No they don't.

CHASE: Sure they do.

GRAY: You don't know.

CHASE: People just don't *not talk* to people.

GRAY: Just because I got caught with the rubberbands.

CHASE: Rubberbands?

GRAY: A big blob of rubberbands. I couldn't help it.

CHASE: Caught doing what exactly?

(GRAY *sits on the sofa.)*

GRAY: I was putting them down my pants.

CHASE: Whoa.

GRAY: Sometimes I'll grab a handful. When my boss isn't looking.

CHASE: Oh. What does that like um *do*?

GRAY: It takes the loneliness away.

CHASE: Huh.

GRAY: I think about the woods sometimes. Just getting away from it all. The smell of deer. Big timber. Blackbirds in the branches.

(Pause)

CHASE: Go get your T V, Gray.

GRAY: Okay. *(He rises, crosses to the front door, turns back.)* Maybe I could just leave it up here, you know? Then I could come up and visit whenever.

CHASE: Hey, it's definitely worth discussing.

GRAY: Okay. *(He turns to exit.)*

CHASE: What kinda T V is it?

GRAY: Magnavox nineteen-inch stereo surroundsound with master remote.

CHASE: The kinda remote that's like heavy in your hand?

GRAY: Uh-huh.

CHASE: Totally go get it.

GRAY: Okay.

CHASE: But Gray?

GRAY: Yeah?

(CHASE *moves himself to an upright position, feigning great pain. As before,* GRAY *reaches awkwardly, feebly, to help him, falls to his knees. Then suddenly, his hands find*

CHASE's *hair, his face, his beard. It's more about the relief of physical human connection than anything sexual. Nonetheless, another awkward moment)*

CHASE: Promise me you'll be careful.

GRAY: I will, Chase. *(He rises, crosses to the door, stops, and turns back one more time.)* Um. I've never told anyone about that before.

CHASE: About what?

GRAY: The rubberband thing. *(He exits.)*

(A moment later, LYNCH enters. There is ice in his beard. He is carrying a small BOY, perhaps six or seven and bundled in a hooded winter parka, scarf, and rollerblades. On the backs of both rollerblades, the name "PETE" is spelled out in colorful decals. He is not wearing pants. One of his legs is discolored. His arms hang lifelessly at his sides. LYNCH is still wearing his snowmobile suit. He is also holding a black garbage bag containing a few lightweight objects.)

LYNCH: Hey.

CHASE: Hey, dude... Who's that?

LYNCH: Pete.

CHASE: Oh. Where's he from?

LYNCH: The park.

CHASE: Like the *park* park?

LYNCH: Uh-huh.

CHASE: What were you doing in the park?

LYNCH: Just walkin around.

CHASE: Walkin around, huh?

LYNCH: Pretty much, yeah. The monkey bars were interesting.

CHASE: Is that where you found, um, *Pete*?

LYNCH: He was sleepin up against one of the handball courts. This dog was tryin to mess with him but I took care of that.

CHASE: Where are his, like, pants?

LYNCH: I don't know. *(He starts for the kitchen area.)*

CHASE: Um, Lynch.

LYNCH: *(Stopping)* Yeah?

CHASE: Pete doesn't look too good.

(LYNCH *crosses to the kitchen table, sets the* BOY *in a chair, starts the oven, opens the oven door.*)

CHASE: What are you doin, dude?

LYNCH: Warmin him up.

CHASE: Maybe you should like take him to the hospital.

LYNCH: He's just cold. He'll be okay. *(From the plastic garbage bag he removes two child-made animal masks: one is obviously a bear mask; the other is a half-made elephant mask.)*

CHASE: What are those?

LYNCH: Oh, I think Pete was makin em. This one's a bear. I think the other one's sposed to be an elephant. *(Putting the bear mask on).* Wanna play? You can be the elephant?

CHASE: ...Um, how's your toe, dude?

LYNCH: It's still numb. So is my leg. And I can't feel my knee. *(He unsnaps his outerwear bottoms, pushes them down to his ankles, standing naked now).*

LYNCH: It's still there, right?

CHASE: Yeah, dude, it's still there.

(GRAY *enters with the TV, stops suddenly.*)

GRAY: Hi.

LYNCH: Hi.

GRAY: I'm Gray.

(*Awkward pause*)

CHASE: Gray, this is Lynch.

GRAY: Nice to meet you Lynch.

(LYNCH *doesn't respond, just stands there, still wearing the mask.*)

CHASE: (*Pointing to the* BOY *seated at the kitchen table*) And that's, um, Pete.

(GRAY *is confused.*)

LYNCH: Pete's pretty shy.

(GRAY *places the T V on the floor in front of the other one. He turns to* LYNCH.)

GRAY: You're wearing a bear mask.

LYNCH: Yeah.

GRAY: And you're naked.

LYNCH: Oh. Sorry. (*He pulls his pants up, stands there.*)

(GRAY *plugs in the T V, attaches the cable box, removes a large remote from his breast pocket, crosses to* CHASE, *almost hands it to him, then starts for the door.*)

CHASE: Where you goin, Gray?

(GRAY *looks at* LYNCH, *then back to* CHASE.)

GRAY: Um. They called me when I was downstairs.

CHASE: They.

GRAY: *Them.*

CHASE: The "money dudes"?

(GRAY *looks at* LYNCH, *and then* CHASE.)

GRAY: *(Careful)* The call was in reference to that certain *government official* I was telling you about. They need me.

CHASE: They like *need you* need you?

GRAY: They sounded professionally desperate.

CHASE: For the "money job"?

GRAY: *(Finally handing* CHASE *the remote)* It's a Mission, yes. I have to go pack my knives. I shouldn't say anything else.

CHASE: Right.

GRAY: And I can't forget my hat. Gotta go. *(He is frozen.)*

CHASE: Gray.

GRAY: Yes?

CHASE: Maybe you should take a pill.

(GRAY *crosses to the bowl of pills.)*

GRAY: You think?

CHASE: Oh, absolutely.

GRAY: Which one?

CHASE: Take a pink.

(GRAY *takes a pink pill from the bowl, pops it in his mouth, then removes a nondescript mint green plastic bottle from his breast pocket, unscrews it, drinks, washing down the pill.)*

CHASE: Take two, dude.

(GRAY *takes another pink, washes it down.)*

CHASE: Take a yellow, too.

(GRAY *takes a yellow, washes it down, returns the bottle to his breast pocket.)*

CHASE: That should do it.

GRAY: If you don't see me anymore I want you to have the T V.

CHASE: Okay.

GRAY: It's good to feel like you're a part of something. *(He exits, closes the door.)*

LYNCH: So you don't wanna be the elephant?

CHASE: Not right now.

LYNCH: You sure?

CHASE: Pretty sure, dude.

LYNCH: Okay.

(LYNCH *crosses to the* BOY, *lifts him out of the chair, starts for the back of the apartment with him.*)

CHASE: Lynch.

LYNCH: Yeah?

CHASE: What are you gonna like do with, um, Pete?

LYNCH: I was gonna play him a song.

CHASE: Oh.

LYNCH: But first I'm gonna clean him. He's pretty dirty.

CHASE: Right on.

(LYNCH *exits down the hall with the* BOY.)

(*Moments later, the window is opened.* STAPLES *climbs through with a large MacDonald's bag in his mouth. He no longer wears his hat and his snowsuit has been partly blown off. He is bare-chested. There is ice in his hair and beard. He closes the window, barricades the window with the kitchen table, turns to* CHASE.)

STAPLES(*As if caught in a blizzard*)
SNOW
SNOW AND ICE
SNOW AND ICE AND WIND

SLEET IN THE TREES
BIRDS FALLING TO THE PAVEMENT
FROZEN PIGEONS ALL ACROSS TENTH STREET
SO COLD THEY LOOK BLUE
FROST CRAWLING UP THE SIDES OF BUILDINGS
PEOPLE IN FRONT OF THEIR WINDOWS WEARING
COATS SCARVES
SKI MASKS
THE MOON LOOKS LIKE A HUGE ICEBALL

(STAPLES *tosses* CHASE *his Happy Meal box, takes a seat on the stage left end of the sofa, removes his own Happy Meal box, emptying the contents onto his lap.*)

(SPEED *enters from the back of the apartment wearing a welding mask, still in his underwear, holding a power stapler.* STAPLES *hands him his Happy Meal box.* CHASE *hands his to* SPEED *as well.* SPEED *thrusts the Happy Meal boxes into the air victoriously, then crosses to the Happy Meal wall, offers the new additions to the Happy Meal gods, stapling them to the wall.*)

(CHASE *and* STAPLES *don't eat, but simply play with the toys contained inside.*)

(CHASE *uses the remote, finds his channel on the T V. Once again, the sound of the animal being tortured.* CHASE *and* STAPLES *are instantly mesmerized.*)

(LYNCH *enters from the back of the apartment in long underwear. He is no longer wearing the bear mask. There is a large knitting needle sticking out of his right foot. He is carrying* PETE, *who has been bathed and is now dressed in a "LESS: LESS IS MORE" T-shirt and the elephant mask.*)

(CHASE *and* STAPLES *have fallen asleep. Still holding* PETE, LYNCH *watches the T V for a moment, then crosses to* GRAY's *T V, rears back and kicks it in with his needled foot.* CHASE *and* STAPLES *continue sleeping.* SPEED *is seated in the corner now, his welding mask up.*)

(LYNCH *crosses to the keyboard, taps on* SPEED's *welding mask. After no response he bends down, removes an electric guitar from under a heap of debris, hugs it to his chest while singing to* PETE:)

LYNCH: *(Singing)* the element man
collecting noble gases
monatomic plan
helium scam
argon passes

he's got a distance machine
powered by rocket fuel
he's got a color T V
and some microwave tea
to navigate his reprieve

distance, area and volume
space so hard to find

(LYNCH *collapses, slowly gets to his feet. He crosses to the sofa, gathers* PETE *in his arms. Lights fade to a rich blue out.*)

(*Bottomside's* 40 Holes and 40 Goals *plays. During the song,* LYNCH *dances with* PETE. *It's a childlike waltz. He turns a few slow circles throughout the apartment. The dance eventually leads to the hallway and then to the back of the apartment.* STAPLES *wakes, watches* LYNCH *make his way to the back of the apartment with the* BOY.)

there's a hole
in my head
there's a hole
in my pocket
there's a hole
in the floor
there's a hole
in the door
i'm gonna find it
i'm gonna fill it

(The light grows very dark and strange on the window. After a moment he rises off the sofa, finds an old, discarded T-shirt, puts it on, crosses to the window, which is now completely covered with frost.)

there's a hole
in my mattress
there's a hole
in my hand
there's a hole
in the afternoon
there's a hole
in the room
i'm gonna find it
i'm gonna fill it
there's a hole

(STAPLES reaches out and touches the window. He withdraws his hand, and crosses to GRAY's T V. He bends down and puts his hand through the hole, retracts it, stares at his hand, turns to the bowl of pills. He reaches in and takes a blue. Then another. Then another. Then several more. He swallows them all. He takes a pink. Swallows. And then a yellow. STAPLES swallows the pills, slowly and deliberately, staring out.)

there's a hole
in the window
there's a hole
in the wall
there's a hole
in my shower
there's a hole
in the hour
i'm gonna find it
i'm gonna fill it...

(STAPLES returns to the sofa, removes a tulip from the vase, still standing, grabs it, regards it for a moment and then starts to eat the petals one by one while turning a slow circle.)

(After he has eaten all the petals, he sits in his spot on the sofa, leans back, staring out.)

huh-huh-huh
huh-huh-huh...

(STAPLES closes his eyes.)

(The blue light slowly changes to a strange pink light on STAPLES.)

(The song ends.)

(Lights fade to black.)

(Lights slowly fade up.)

(The apartment is filled with yellow light.)

(It is now morning.)

(As before, CHASE *and* STAPLES *are asleep on the couch,* STAPLES *holding the stem of the eaten tulip.)*

(SPEED is back on the floor, now asleep, still wearing the welding mask.)

(A cell phone rings four times, then ceases.)

(LYNCH enters from the back of the apartment. He wears his long underwear. The areas of his shins, arms, forehead, thighs, face, and hands are grotesquely bloody. There are several needles sticking out of his foot. He is carrying his brick.)

(A cell phone rings again.)

(LYNCH stops, turns toward the sound of the cell phone. He leans over CHASE, grabs his cell phone, answers it.)

LYNCH: Hello?... Lynch... Hey, Mister Fitzsimmons... Yeah, he's here, but he's sleepin... Sure, I'll give him a message... Okay... Bye.

(LYNCH *turns the phone off, places it next to* CHASE. *He stares at him a moment, then shakes him.* CHASE *stirs, wakes.*)

CHASE: Hey, Lynch.

LYNCH: Hey. Your dad called.

CHASE: When?

LYNCH: Just now.

CHASE: Oh. What'd he want?

LYNCH: He said he heard about the storm.

CHASE: What storm.

LYNCH: The snowstorm. He just wanted to let you know he heard about it.

(*A beat*)

CHASE: Dude, what happened?

LYNCH: What.

CHASE: You're all bloody.

LYNCH: I woke up in the middle of the night and this robot was hitting me with the brick... But I took care of him... There's metal everywhere back there...

(*The brick falls to the floor.* LYNCH *collapses, expires.*)

(GRAY *enters. He is wearing the same gray suit and tie and an odd-shaped bowler hat. He is wet with snow. He is holding a bloody knife. There blood and vomit on the front of his suit. He is shivering.*)

GRAY: Hi.

CHASE: Hey Gray.

GRAY: Hi. (*He stands very still.*)

GRAY: It's really cold out. Lots of snow.

CHASE: You're holding a knife, dude.

GRAY: Yeah.

CHASE: And there's like blood on it.

GRAY: When it goes in it feels like nothing. It's so light. Even. Like nowhere. You think there will be screaming. Fighting. Music in the background. Like on T V. But it's not like that. Not if you put it in the way they show you. In the part where the voice makes a noise. It was so quiet. And he just sat down. He just sat down like he was old and tired. Like he'd walked for a long time and needed to rest...
   It's so good to feel like you're a part of something. *(He crosses to the tulips, gathers them in his arms.)*

GRAY: My lamp broke. I knocked it over when I unplugged the T V. Broke into a thousand pieces. It's really cold down there. *(He starts to weep)* Can I stay up here with you? I'll be really still. Just a few days.

CHASE: Sure, Gray, sure.

GRAY: I won't move, hardly at all.

CHASE: No problem buddy.

GRAY: I heard the Sun's coming. *(He slowly crosses to the beer sign, steps onto the chair, turns it on. His movements are very slow, as though he is coming to some kind of expiration. He turns the sign on and starts to arrange the tulips in the light over the following:)*

CHASE: *(To* GRAY*)* I had this dream last night...I was a robot... Big metal robot...I was crying but nothing was coming out... No tears... And I didn't have any balls... Instead I had a light switch...I kept trying to turn it on but all it did was make this buzzing noise... *(He plants his feet on the floor for the first time, slowly stands, takes in the room for a moment.)*

(STAPLES' *cell phone starts to ring.* CHASE *thinks it's his. He checks. It's not. He turns to* STAPLES *at the other end of the sofa.*)

(*The cell phone rings again.*)

(CHASE *reaches over, shakes him.* STAPLES *doesn't stir.*)

(CHASE *touches his cheek, draws his hand back, quickly retreats to his side of the sofa.*)

(GRAY *continues to stare at the tulips arranged in the beer light.*)

CHASE: I...I can't feel my feet.

(*Lights fade to black.*)

(*Lights up.*)

(SPEED *is sitting on the sofa, wearing clothes and holding a cassette recorder. He is listening to a recording of a song they have been working on. He and* CHASE *ad lib a bit and then* STAPLES *enters from the bathroom, fanning the air in front of him because he has just committed the worst kind of bathroom crime. They banter a bit and then* LYNCH *enters through the front door with a six-pack of beer. He passes the beer out and then after some bantering they all tune up and turn their amps on and prepare to play a song, which* SPEED *will record with his cassette player.* CHASE *plays the electric guitar.* STAPLES *is at the mic.* SPEED *is at the drums.* LYNCH *is wearing a bass guitar.* STAPLES *starts to sing* **The Astronaut's Lament**. *It starts slowly and then builds into an up-beat pop-song, then opens up into aggressive punk rock. By the end it should be animated, punk rock chaos, all for each other, all for this one perfect moment.*)

STAPLES: (*Singing*)
in the very tiny hours
when the night turns into the day
when your spaceships come

and steal your plans
and make your blue skies change to gray

i sit alone in my room
how can i be so lazy
when the astronauts are giving it one more try
why does the stratosphere look so hazy?

22 days ago
i saw a number cruncher lookin at me
he had a bowling ball tied to his bum left leg
and he walked into the sea

and he went down, down, down, down
down to the end of the pier

he jumped and drowned, drowned, drowned, drowned
but he couldn't get there from here

the junk dealer's getting his fix
the radio ain't playing songs
the kid downstairs is wearing my 3-piece suit
should I make my body strong?

the chief of police lost his gun
the subway map is missing a stop
the rifle dealer's taking a cigarette break
i wonder what he's got in stock?

my corduroy pants are too small
i think my dog is runnin away
if the eskimos can build a house outta snow
then maybe I can build one with hay

and he went down, down, down, down
down to the end of the pier

he jumped and drowned, drowned, drowned, drowned
but he couldn't get there from here

(The song slows down suddenly. A "freak-out"

(The whole of it turns into an extended jam session with inspired improvisation. After a minute or so, they find the bass line and return to the chorus.)

and he went down, down, down, down
down to the end of the pier

he jumped and drowned, drowned, drowned, drowned
but he couldn't get there from here

(On the final run of the drums, before the crash of the symbols, the band freezes in a strobe of white light.)

END OF PLAY

www.ingramcontent.com/pod-product-compliance
Lightning Source LLC
Chambersburg PA
CBHW060221050426
42446CB00013B/3136